Salam to Gaza
The refugee camp lacks bread now
But it is enriched with blood

mpT
MODERN POETRY IN TRANSLATION
The best of world poetry

No. 2 2024
© *Modern Poetry in Translation* 2024 and contributors

ISSN (print) 0969-3572
ISSN (online) 2052-3017
ISBN (print) 978-1-910485-39-2

Editor: Janani Ambikapathy
Managing Editor: Sarah Hesketh
Digital Content Editor: Ed Cottrell
Finance Manager: Deborah de Kock
Creative Apprentice: Chloe Elliott

Design by Brett Evans Biedscheid
Cover Art by Justin Moore
Typesetting by Libanus Press
Proofreading by Katy Evans-Bush

Printed and bound in Great Britain by Typecast Colour, Kent.
For submissions and subscriptions please visit
www.modernpoetryintranslation.com

Modern Poetry in Translation Limited. A Company Limited by Guarantee
Registered in England and Wales, Number 5881603 UK
Registered Charity Number 1118223

Supported using public funding by
ARTS COUNCIL
ENGLAND
LOTTERY FUNDED

Cover description: Cover shows a collage of images of individuals engaged in gestures of protest. Some hold placards, one shouts through a megaphone. The bottom right shows a car which has been set alight.

Above: On the left, the Arts Council England logo curves around in a circle, next to a black outline of a hand crossing fingers. Underneath both images, 'LOTTERY FUNDED' is written. In a line on the right, the text reads, 'Supported using public funding by ARTS COUNCIL ENGLAND'.

MODERN POETRY IN TRANSLATION

Salam to Gaza:
Focus on Resistance

CONTENTS

'My front façade is autumn'

EDITORIAL

by Janani Ambikapathy, Editor

Recently, standing in front of Pieter Bruegel the Elder's 'Landscape with the Flight into Egypt', at the Courtauld gallery, my friend and I were discussing Raymond Geuss's argument about the moral choice of locating oneself in a painting as opposed to being a viewer. The question is: should we see ourselves as the characters in the painting, take a side, or maybe even implicate ourselves?

I wondered if the predicament applies to poetry. We're all sophisticated enough to know that the 'you' isn't you, and the 'I' isn't I, but could we, as readers, locate ourselves in a poem? This is to go further than merely identifying with an emotion or a sensibility. Choosing a position in the poem would be akin to choosing a position in the world: viewer or participant?

One of the more difficult things about living a life can be working out who we are within the structures that control us, and arriving at a political position that can emancipate us and others. It is surprising to me that poetry (or even painting) is not one of the common means to this end. A thought experiment like no other – a poem, if you allow it, can change your mind.

If you were to choose to participate in a poem from this issue – perhaps it is a poem from Gaza, by Batool Abu Akleen, about the genocidal acts being committed by the Israeli forces, or a poem by Jacinta Kerketta from India, about resisting the assault of the Indian state on its indigenous people – you may (or may not) act differently in the world outside the poem. But having made a choice in the poem, to support two liberation struggles, you have in front of you several possible courses of action: you can join the BDS campaign, find out more about Gautam Adani, or support Fossil Free Books, amongst other things. Even if you choose not to act immediately, the possibilities of your life are now different: you just

imagined a different world order through the poem, alongside
millions of people.

I'm less interested in the question 'can art change the world?' – it is
too vast and generic to elicit a useful answer. The better approach is to
think about the distance between ourselves and the work of art. Every
poem in this issue, then, is an invitation to read with stakes in the game.

As I expected, a focus on 'dissent and resistance' had the submission
inbox brimming with poems – we received a far greater number than
we can possibly publish. Usually, each issue consists of a general
section, and a separate set of poems in the 'focus' section. In the
current issue, we decided to break with tradition and keep our
attention trained on dissent, to emphasise its ongoing necessity in
the present historical moment.

We'll begin with Palestine, and travel eastwards: a poem by Hussein
Barghouthi – the title of this issue takes a line from the poem –
translated from Arabic by Suneela Mubayi, and poems by Batool Abu
Akleen, translated from Arabic by the author and Cristina Viti.
Speaking after Barghouthi, we say our 'Salam' to Gaza. Abd al-Karim
al-Ahmad writes from Syria, translated by Catherine Cobham from
Arabic, about the inconsolable horrors experienced by migrants at the
threshold of fortress Europe. Missak Manouchian was an intrepid
Armenian anti-fascist and communist; he makes an appearance in
English for the very first time, translated from Western Armenian by

Opposite: In black and white, various photographs of various former
MPT contributors in three rows of six. Below are the MPT logo and
motto, 'The best of world poetry', and a quote from John Berger, saying
'ANYONE WHO WANTS TO CHANGE THE WORLD AND SEE
IT CHANGED SHOULD JOIN MPT'. Below that is the ACE logo,
as well as a line describing MPT, our social media information,
website, and subscription information (£29 a year – UK Subscription,
£44 – International Subscription).

Jennifer Manoukian. Shahin Shirzadi writes from Iran, translated from Persian by Ali Asadollahi, about the guilt and fear of being on the sidelines of protests. Asadollahi says, '[...] but they are scared, because the bullet is real, and it goes through the flesh. It's no joke.' Onward to South Asia, where Jacinta Kerketta writes deceptively candid poems, translated from Hindi by Bhumika Chawla-D'Souza, catching the Indian state at its most duplicitous. Avinash Shrestha writes with an incendiary spirit from Nepal, and his poems have been translated from Nepali by Rohan Chhetri. Crossing over into China, Jike Ayou, a migrant worker writes exquisite poems, translated from Chinese by Yě Yě, about watching the seasons pass from the airless factory floor. Afrizal Malna's 'polyvocal prose poems' from Indonesia, translated from Indonesian by Daniel Owen, layer the streets of Jakarta with facts and abstractions. Then there are poems by Jorge Lauten from Timor-Leste, translated from Portuguese by Shook, a pseudonymous revolutionary who might be you.

In South Korea, a prescient Yi Sang, translated from Korean by Jack Saebyok Jung, takes us through an unsettling, war-torn landscape. From Chile, Raúl Zurita, translated by Jessica Sequeira from Spanish, writes movingly about the 'dream of the maddening possibility of happiness' – there is something to be said about the 'possibility' itself being a dream in the current moment. Leo Boix translates the Mapuche poet Liliana Ancalao from Spanish, whose piercing poems remind us of the struggle of the indigenous people made all that much harder by the newly elected head of state in Argentina.

We move further east into Africa, Côte d'Ivoire to be precise, to read poems by Henri-Michel Yéré, translated from French and Nouchi by Todd Fredson. It is an honour to introduce a new language, Nouchi, to the MPT canon. The poems read like a fever dream taken hostage by the police when Yéré snaps us out of it:

'how to displace / a person already adrift'. There are more poems ahead from Italy, Germany, Ukraine, Romania and Hungary.

I'm against ahistorical nostalgia, loath to imagine a false pre-colonial paradise – but I do think about the languages we would have read each other in if English hadn't become the lingua franca. We might have possessed various levels of expertise in many languages, and not strained towards a *single* language that has come to define our literary acumen. I hope that on a hill somewhere beyond English, these poems full of rage and liberatory desire are as intelligible as in the native tongue.

I'm so grateful to my colleagues, Sarah, Ed and Debbie for supporting me through the errors and the missteps committed in putting together my very first issue. My gratitude to Justin Moore for the brilliant cover design – a collage is, after all, translation's alter ego.

In solidarity,
Janani

A note from the cover artist, Justin Moore: 'I have been particularly intrigued by collage for its accessible nature, its archival connections to the past, and the practice's grounding in notions of sustainability and 'upcycling'. As we approach a more paperless landscape, wherein modes of action and interaction are becoming increasingly more digitised, I view paper collage as a form of resistance. I consider the manipulation and re-contextualisation of existing images as a resistance against the stagnation of ideas, a resistance against the squandering of the material, and a resistance against an original image's loss to the passage of time. While digital collage may be subject to fewer constraints, it is also of particular interest to me, as evidenced by this issue's cover.'

'But someone
has shattered
too'

JIKE AYOU

Translated by Yě Yě from Chinese

Jike Ayou was born in the beautiful mountains of Puge county in China's Sichuan province, where over 86 per cent of the population is of Yi ethnicity. He worked a number of factory jobs in the east of the country before becoming a professional writer and poet.

These poems, chosen from his book of poetry *All of Our Homecomings Are Feted as Yi New Year* (Taibai Literature and Art Publishing House, 2019), attest to Ayou's struggles as a migrant worker living in poor conditions, receiving unfair wages, and lacking recreational opportunities.

Through these brief yet sharp lines, Ayou draws a picture of his everyday life as a migrant worker and poet: the melancholic sound of jaw harp (a traditional Yi folk instrument) which kindles his homesickness on a sleepless night, the naive dreaming of innocent love that riots after long shifts, and the scorching image of perennially dwarfed workers as they erect the skyscrapers of the modernity.

Are the cicadas merely the mad grievers of a passing season? Or are they the singing spirit of relentlessness even as they near the end of their journey?

As a translator, it is my duty to convey these struggles as precisely as possible without any loss of referential subtleties.

sound of a jaw harp in the labelling factory

the folk songs tonight, sounding rather unusual
suddenly flame my withering ears

the labelling factory has no licence, exhaust or ventilation system
yet it's got my little teenage cousin

beside a box oven, she who reads not a single word
knows how to smear paints into the English letters on a mould

Opposite: Jike Ayou

the construction site at the Beginning of Autumn[1]

it's the Beginning of Autumn, cicadas lament August over and over
there's a breeze from the treetops
i shelter in the shade

over the construction site, tawny skinned, they gulp the cheap tea
the entire summer in their cracked mouths
the buildings are taller every day
they smaller, like an army of ants
climbing up the scaffold, hovering still in the air

1 'Beginning of Autumn' is the first solar term of autumn in the traditional Chinese calendar.

factory in the summer

the more the peach blossoms wither, the shorter the skirts
　　of female workers get
those areas that shouldn't be exposed
are groped by men's glances

this factory in the summer
fans blowing a riot of hot air
some people dream of passionate love
some a casual affair
therefore something irrelevant to assembly lines
is peddled at the crossroads of nightshifts, though its voice
slighter than that of the fried noodle seller, pancake maker,
　　watermelon vendor, and pineapple cutter
someone would always throw a note, five, ten or twenty yuan,
and disappear like a thief
the humming of insects is dull no more
lights in the dormitory rooms sleep early

HENRI-MICHEL YÉRÉ

Translated by Todd Fredson from French and Nouchi

The poems are excerpted from the collection *Polo kouman/Polo parle* by Henri-Michel Yéré. The book was a finalist for the 2023 Grand Prix Littéraire d'Afrique Noire. Part of what is compelling about the collection, and part of its dissent, is that the poems are written in both French and Nouchi. Nouchi is a language aggregated out of French, West African languages, onomatopoeias, slang, etc.; it began in the 1970s as an immigrant 'pidgin' dialect but has become so widely used as to be considered its own language. Yéré has written each poem in *Polo kouman/Polo parle* twice. Neither language is more original than the other; neither is more authoritative, per se – which should I translate from? That question of linguistic authority is central to the book.

Polo, the protagonist, is a young man born and bred in Abidjan, Côte d'Ivoire. He's seen the rougher side of Abidjanais life; he speaks Nouchi because he's a child of the street. The name 'Polo' is a nod to John Pololo, who was a legendary figure of Abidjan's street life in the 1980s and 1990s. Pololo was a rebellious figure, one of the inventors of the dancing style known as gnaman-gnaman, yet also a thug unofficially employed by President Houphouët-Boigny. The president used him and his friends to break student demonstrations regularly. Polo speaks to *Demain/Devant* – in other words, his own future – and *Demain* speaks back. Words are like weapons in Polo's mouth, and *Demain/Devant* matches his tone. Therefore, they clash. The poems here are from three of the book's four sections.

Opposite: Henri-Michel Yéré

from *1: Polo Speaks*

It is from the margins that we left
to invade the paper
like that paved route from Attécoubé

We are roughshod

The rain has done what it could
to pulp our notebooks

The city's lines blur

Diesel has declared war on the sky
The cloud is white as a weapon

Come to Earth to face the lions
we fell into the wrong jungle

we blindfold ourselves
we cross the highway

we are the only ones who know Tomorrow's address

when the Round-up[1] arrives
we'll wrestle

hands against claws
prey against hunters

daybreak dulled by hissing violence

in this jungle-festooned trench

---

1 There is one historic round-up, dating back to 1983, which Alpha Blondy evokes
in his famous tune 'Brigadier Sabari'. The capitalised 'R' in this context is a way
of evoking in one word the police, their brutality, and these round-ups, which
have long been used to disrupt street life and its required daily hustle.

from 2: *The Truth of Tomorrow*

I see the place you were born, by the water.

The waves, always about to flood the land. Your
quarrel with the lagoon is old; whoever would pull you out
is not yet born.

Rain adds itself to the lagoon, and your parent's shack
standing as well as it can crumbles into the ground
a little bit more. Every rainy season, you moved.
Around that same patch of land...

And then there were the bulldozers –

You were the first to understand the language of the bull-
dozers. Amid the rampage, they never saw you.
You went to your secret lair; you hid inside
of yourself. Big dilemma, for a bulldozer: how to displace
a person already adrift.

from 3: *The Clash*

I replaced my blood with lava;
no one took my salivations seriously.

My pride towered over me:
I came to undress life.

Chock-full with madness' sap the herbs
arranged the name Tomorrow.

Amid the sharp knives
and the shining bullets,
I would have wished for a beacon,
some improvised act;
during the drowning, a buoy,

or, even just to get right to it,
that much-feared clash.

Tomorrow, too quickly you decreed
that we were sons of shopkeepers,
sons of cooks, maids,
little Fantines, seasonal help –

you think our words
sound like barking?

You're getting ahead of yourself.
Lifted from the bed of speech,
words have opened a way.

The speaking remains our peril –
here we are dancing in your head –
let's get your tongue out of that vaulted throne room.

AFRIZAL MALNA

Translated by Daniel Owen from Indonesian

These poems come from Afrizal Malna's 2002 book *No Dog in My Mother's Womb*, which collects poems written between 1997 and 2001. This was a time of social upheaval and transition in Malna's native Jakarta that saw the devastating economic effects of the 1997 financial crisis, coupled with the mass social movement for democratic reform, contributing to the fall of General Suharto's 32-year New Order military dictatorship in May 1998. In the poems gathered here, we find a poetics of slanted witness, an imaginative depiction of the sociopolitical scenes playing out on the streets of Jakarta and the environs rendered through a shifting series of images, utterances, and facts.

No Dog in My Mother's Womb is something of a culmination of the heavily repetitious, polyvocal prose poem style of his 90s work. Afrizal describes his method of this period as one of 'thinking in images' rather than thinking in concepts, a practice of collage-like recontextualisation of words and their associations intended to help break out of the authoritarian tendencies inherent in language, tendencies that were especially exacerbated by the New Order's attempts at totalitarian thought control through linguistic and cultural policy.

No Dog in My Mother's Womb also signals a turning point in Malna's life and writing. Following its publication, he stepped away from the world of literature for several years to work as an activist with the Urban Poor Consortium, a nongovernmental organisation that supports Jakarta's urban poor in their struggle for self-determination in the face of developmentalist policies that threaten their livelihoods and homes.

Workers' Flame and Insurance for Toys

November 13, 1970, who made me into a worker, who created me to be a worker. My name is Chun Tae Il, a man and a worker in my self. Each day when I come home from the factory, the sweat of my people flows through my body. But there's no nationalism in a factory. November 13, 1970, at the Seoul Peace Market, I drenched that body in kerosene and sparked a flame. That flame torched the body, as though burning the sweat of my people. A sun burst from my body, from its spark. People spilled into the streets, out from every door, to witness a workers' protest written on the soul of that spark. I am the spirit of Asia for every worker's oppression.

1991, that year, my name is Mi Kyong, a woman and worker from Korea. I jumped from a tall building and died, my name is Mi Kyong, a woman and a worker. On my arm I wrote a message: 'Bury me in your heart, not in this cold, tortuous country.' The years pass, the workers expend their time in factories. Our lungs, our blood, our wombs have become nests of poison, with no insurance. The factory takes the whole of our lives. Who made me into a worker and who built the factory, transforming earth and sea into a motor. Who is playing with international finance and convulsing time's backbone. Who plays with fire and burns their own face.

1993, in Thailand, the Kader factory, which produced toys, burnt down. The emergency exit doors were locked. The key lit up, hanging in the sky. Why were the emergency exit doors locked. Why build a factory as a killing box. Time too melted in the blaze. 188 workers killed in the flames. There's no insurance for workers. But there is insurance for toys. The factory was rebuilt. The toys were rebuilt. But the dead workers could never live again. The blazing flame kept burning, becoming the flame of Asia. The flame of Asia that opens every factory gate. Feet of fire that move to make the date on your desk.

Politics' Corpse Covered with the Morning Paper

Someone has disappeared. But someone has shattered too. The president is in the hospital. His hands and throat spout saws. But the house of representatives must be rebuilt. Like building a sun from banana leaves. Someone has disappeared. The earth pukes up their body. Soldiers' boots spill from their mouth. Someone has disappeared. A corpse stink permeates the parliament building, the kitchen too. The president must be rebuilt. The cabinet must be rebuilt. But someone has disappeared. A politics made of saws covers their eyes. The earth pukes. No longer can it yield plants. Someone has shattered. The plants puke. No longer can they bear fruit. The forest burns itself down. Buildings burn themselves down. Someone burns, is burnt down. Someone is raped. The country is raped. Someone has disappeared, I kidnap myself. Parliament must be built. A student relinquishes their body before the dictator button. Someone has disappeared! Burnt corpse. A faith that stores corpses. Some language threatens your throat. A shattered faith. Children can't drink milk, can't go to school. Books too pricey. Paddy fields no longer bear fruit. Some volcano erupts. The people must be built. Demos must be built. Some torture site. Bones dug from your throat. The doors of parliament sawed open. Some sun, softly, built from banana leaves. Come here. Listen. This country is for you. Don't look at me like that. I'm a corpse. A corpse of politics. I was kidnapped. Tortured. Don't bury me like that, like burying this country. Don't. Come here. Listen. This is my hand. Still warm. Like a bandage of politics to cover your eyes. Come here. Come. Still have another hundred years in this place, here, on this land.

1998

Rain from a Kitchen

I just bought some crackers and cucumbers. Your eyes carried me.
And the rice is cooked. I rode a bike to bring it home. And your voice
rode a bike to the hill. On your breast an orange tree grows. Wind
blows there often, like your backpack that carries rain. The earth
never stops birthing plants. And the morning sun, all of dawn, for
those who don't yet have a country of their own. Come on, dear,
Pak Daman is waiting, and Ibu Entin and company, at the Selamat
Datang Monument roundabout. The banners and posters are ready.
The hands of the poor that make the earth fertile. They want to plant
an orange tree, speak to the soldiers about throats turned blue and
the hand of god taking to the streets. They move with feet of rain.
Their breath fragrant with the scent of orange. Not the stink of the
soldiers in Timor-Leste who trade their eyes for iron stars.

— *Aceh, take your own language for resistance.*

With every hand that learns to hold, human stench's search for its
country grows more steadfast.

ATTILA JÓZSEF

Translated by Ágnes Lehóczky and Adam Piette
from Hungarian

These translations are part of a longer project to translate a
significant selection of the poems of the modernist, socialist,
working-class Hungarian poet, Attila József (1905–1937), one of the
most celebrated and loved poets of the 20th century in Hungary.
After a difficult childhood scarred by the early death of his mother,
he became a communist, was expelled from university for his
scandalously radical poems, then from the Communist Party for his
interest in psychoanalysis. He lived a poverty-stricken, passionate
and unstable life as a wanderer, poet and lover till his untimely death
by suicide, struck by a train, in Balatonszárszó on Lake Balaton,
aged only 32. His poetry is surrealist, Villonesque, tough-minded,
passionate, lyrical, marked by his solitary wandering, his keen
observation of the lives of the people, by his psychoanalytically
inflected gaze into the unconscious, into the mind and body of
lovers. The lyrics, free verse and formal, in an astonishing number
of experimental forms, range from the metaphysical to the memoir,
have filiations to French mediaeval, post-symbolist and surrealist
poetry, fuse Marx and Freud in daring raids on the inarticulate, sing
with haunting beauty and rise to extraordinary heights and flights of
the imagination, yet are always grounded in the real, in the concrete
particulars of the metropolis, the dark streets of the underclasses of
this world.

There, I've found my home at last

There, I've found my home at last,
this patch of land where you will find
my name carved out, and no mistake.
(if they bury me, someone kind).

Land like a poor box: clink I'm in,
a rusty tuppence, crude, worn-down,
one no-one wants, a gloomy, war-
blasted and useless, clapped-out coin;

and not the ring so fine inscribed
with words that sing of brave new world,
law and land: Obey wartime rules,
gold rings gleam brighter, worth accrued.

I lived on my own such a long time –
though lots of people came to hang
out, saying, shame you live apart,
happy if I'd been one of their gang.

That's how I lived, lived pointlessly –
I assume and suspect they made
me play the fool all that damned time,
and my death, too, useless and crude.

All my life lived in a whirlwind,
standing upright in stormblast I tried.
Don't understand how I didn't cause
more harm than the harm I endured.

Spring is lovely, summer's fine,
autumn's finer, winter's best. Brothers
and a warm fire: dying wish,
not for himself, but for all others.

'Íme, hát megleltem hazámat', November, 1937

Go little song

Go little song, speak little song,
to each and every one of us,
sing we're alive, can hope and long,
box time's ears, so there's time for us.

Calm the souls of the panicky rich,
tell them we'll show them all mercy.
Love and freedom water their ditch
with purest water not blood, see?

Speak, as through the calf's droopy mouth,
to the hard-working masses, the poor –
tell them in searing words the truth,
they need act the hero no more.

'Szállj költemény', early March, 1937

KI-TYO SSEMMA'NDA

Translated by the poet from Luganda

I have translated the Ugandan experience and speech pattern from the Luganda language through the 'eye' of the common man. I'm interested in how they look at issues that concern them. Usually, their response is penned in a matter-of-fact tone – they are disillusioned, scared or devoid of hope.

The common man in Uganda is reminded of his 'country' constantly, and yet the services that are vital never arrive. The Ugandan national motto is 'For God and my country.' Maybe we need to ask ourselves this question again and again: do politicians make a lot of noise?

Girl and Man Disguise

Girl in disguise
wears a fedora to look like fedora man
and leaves home for a mission
Girl hides her great old black face
and twisted sleuth hair spread on face
girl's success worked, hat is in place of dye
girl now looks girl
and fedora man meets girl and
treats girl as girl not woman
but girl is wiser than girl's age,
Girl leaves mission accomplished
and weaves another plan.

man weaves a mission with 27 guns to go to the bush
and live a life of a pauper, cobra and impala
man hides ambition on the pavements of Kampala
and visions away from Uganda and girl
man spreads propaganda of
hatred for opulence and greed
he rewrites history since 1962 –
a role man succeeds. It worked, they say. You're one of us –
man is now a big man
sits at Kololo next to statue of Maloba
with mansions as cars and wealth surround him

It's now 40 full years
And man is seated still, unmoved
He speaks,
'You can't treat Uganda as Uganda,
There's no other plan'
except to treat girl as girl.

Foghorns Deafen Me...

In this Lock-Box, it's easier to stand in aisles where people steal stuff because – it's after all the right place for what's of value and where everything is locked.

To demand service or be heard, I've got to push a button to herald YOU and get help.

And on this old spot where I stand there used to be a 'Medical Care Center' – there's now a button that I press until the foghorn goes unmanageably off: 'THIS IS YOUR COUNTRY, FOR GOD AND MY COUNTRY.'

And I'll wait with the patience of a sick man groaning for a surgeon. But I usually grieve for 5 more years before I can remind them to come over again.

And I place my thumb again when that time elapses. But still they don't heed to my pain. They'll drag their heels or won't come ever. I may well wait anyway, for I'm in need of help.

And to call the tune, who am I? And remember all the things I have not paid in their taxes.

Fortunately a peoples' Piper on A.O.B passes by and spots a figure with a body ncxt to a cardboard wall and asks: 'Do you need help in any way mate?'

My rude sun-dried angry self would have asked, 'Didn't you hear the foghorn madam Piper?'

But since manners for my type are cruel in places of this nature, to toe the line is a thing to do for crumbs – so I code-bend to fit the type with, 'Yes, sir-madam. I need the help to heal and feed and be myself.'

I turn my gaze further in the distance to hide from the faces of their eyes. They walk too, each finger in their ears.

SHAHIN SHIRZADI

Translated by Ali Asadollahi from Persian

As a person who has witnessed and participated in mass peaceful protests that were violently suppressed, I can say that the pattern has always been the same: there are those who voice their demands for water, for land, for freedom, for economy, and then there are those who silently watch and wait for them to win. Eventually, the 'criminal violence' of state which leads to mass murder, torture and prison pushes the fighters back into their shelters and the observers are left with more to fear.

Living in constant fear, traumatised by witnessing the oppression and murder of human beings who have the most natural and human desires, leaves a mark. These visible failures discourage many people from taking to the street and claiming their rights. It doesn't mean that they don't suffer, no, but they are scared, because the bullet is real, and it goes through the flesh. It's no joke. Shahin Shirzadi's poem is an attempt to be the voice of those who look at the events through the window and on the mobile screen, rather than being on the street.

Of Those I'm Not Coming Back From

Of those who know you, I'm just one
Since one of me writes down by turns
Others listen in silence
And I – those others – am not going anywhere from me
I won't come back

One of us had fallen in the street's crack
It is said that she wanted to fly over Tehran
But wings are vital to flight
That one doesn't talk anymore
Fallen
In the street's crack
She listens

Of us, you see the second one   on this branch
You see, she scattered on the branch
Some days you don't have time for your friend to take her down
From far away you can only say her name

One of us was younger
It means, she fell young
Because the soil is enough to fall
We don't know her name
She didn't have a name since she was the first of us
And the first can't be named

Some days
Of the one you know, we are a crowd
Around Towhid Sq, we may scatter or
Near the guardrail of Modarres, we may fall
But instead of wings, we have mouths

One of us is running away in Ferdows
We say her name
One of us is falling in Saqqez
We say her name
And in 14 pt font
Our voice is being put down

Of those you know
We have all been asleep
We have dreamed that our friend rises from the gap between
      the sentences
Takes a new sentence out of her sleeve
A bright sentence
We repeat that sentence in our sleep, not to forget
When we are awake in the dark

What you know of us is scared
Our voice, it's stuttering
But we can say our friend's name, stuttering
We are not going anywhere, we won't come back
We stay here with our stutter
And our stutter stays in the street's crack

'Toward the masses, to offer my soul to the masses once and for all'

HUSSEIN BARGHOUTHI

Translated by Suneela Mubayi from Arabic

Hussein Barghouthi's prose oeuvre is perhaps better known than his poems. Moheeb Barghouthi, a poet and a photographer, and Hussein's cousin, pointed me to this poem, published for the first time this year in the *Journal of Palestine Studies,* as part of a special issue on poets from Gaza. Barghouthi was from Kobar village outside Ramallah, and wrote this poem during the First Intifada in 1987. It was never published in his lifetime. He recorded it on a cassette tape, and it was transcribed by Moheeb; the line breaks and punctuation are therefore the latter's. Reading and re-reading this poem, one can understand why Hussein wanted it preserved as a recording – it is the kind of poem that should be read out aloud to feel its full impact.

The poem is liturgical or hymn-like, but one outside of any specific religious context. It is written in an easy idiom. The key to the poem is the word, 'salam', which is part of the title and the refrain. 'Salam' is one of those Arabic words that has travelled far and wide and has many semantic connotations, depending on how it is used: it could be a simple hello, or used to wish someone health, safety, peace, or serve as a hail or a salute in a comradely sense.

Here Barghouthi seems to be both wishing peace upon Gaza and saluting Gazan people's courage and resilience in confronting the occupier who inflicts death and misery upon them.

Salam to Gaza

My sister will live without me
My family will live without me
Part of me will live without me
The whole of me will live without me.
Salam to those holding out in prison
my heart goes out to those who died inside
A sparrow's peck to those who remain,
Peace be upon a stone, blue like ocean waves
Like the sky, like mountain goats' eyes,
like flights of pigeons, peace be upon that stone,
peace be upon it, upon it
upon it, right now
are the dreams of a land, hopes of a nation
Peace be upon a stone encircled by flowers
That girls' eyes reach out to embrace

Salam to Gaza
The refugee camp lacks bread now
But it is enriched with blood
The camp lacks land and bread
But now it ascends to the skies
Salam to Gaza's doves
Where they flutter they brush at my heart
And drink of my water
To honour those who remain
Silence outdoes words

Salam to a pair of eyelashes on a boy's face
Rafah eyelashes wet with roses and tears
Salam to those offering their bodies to coffin-bearers
And a sparrow's peck to those who remain
What can I offer to the cemetery
The road into it
Is the very road we take to depart it like gods
The massacring hand cannot overpower
the torrents of life
The streets, like the sparrows, stand still
They drink from rain whose free drops come from clouds
     floating free in a free sky
Salam to these trees
Their cry rings louder than my song

MISSAK MANOUCHIAN

Translated by Jennifer Manoukian from Western Armenian

The poems excerpted here are from Missak Manouchian's only poetry collection, *Բանաստեղծութիւններ* [Poems], published posthumously in 1946. These poems – meditations on labour, exploitation and social responsibility – had been written more than a decade earlier, during a period of becoming in Manouchian's life. After his arrival in France in 1924, Manouchian laboured in a variety of industries and experienced firsthand the day-to-day struggles of the working class. When Manouchian wrote these poems in 1933 and 1934, he was at the very beginning of his engagement with the French Communist Party and of his work in support of immigrant workers in France. The sense of injustice, outrage and compassion for the downtrodden that preoccupied and propelled him in this work is on full display in the poems.

Largely unknown outside France, Armenia and pockets of the Armenian diaspora, examples of Manouchian's poetry are appearing here for the first time in English translation. The original poetry collection was translated into French from Western Armenian by Stéphane Cermakian, and published under the title *Ivre d'un grand rêve de liberté* (2024) in celebration of Manouchian's entry into the Panthéon in 2024.

Thank you to Houry Varjabédian at Éditions Parenthèses in Marseille for her kindness in orienting me in the multifaceted life and work of Missak Manouchian.

Opposite: Missak Manouchian

Deprivation

Friends sometimes ask me:
—How is it that you can survive and always, from the depths
    of your soul,
Yearn to give strength to hearts in despair
When you yourself are so often deprived and hungry?

—When wandering along the city streets,
I call on my eyes to collect in my soul
The uninterrupted sighs and pleas
Of immeasurable misery and deprivation.

I blend them with my own suffering;
With the venoms of hate, I prepare
A tart serum that flows like blood
Through all the veins of my body and soul.

This liquid may perhaps seem strange to you,
But it enlivens me, transforms me into a tiger...
My teeth and fists tightly clenched,
I pass through the city streets.

People often think I am crazy or drunk.
While in the agitation of revery,
My thoughts are besieged, looping on their own,
And I proceed with faith toward triumph.

30 June, 1934
Paris

The Cry of the Masses

When, in the solitude of my room,
A heartfelt intimacy grows between the silence, the paper,
   the writing and me
And my mind soars like an eagle,
Up into the past toward the expanse of human history,

Or when, no longer fettered by the venomous bite of worry
Or by the blood-soaked clutches of tedium,
I grow infinitely and blissfully intoxicated
By the sage mysteries of art,

Wild forces turn the course of my soul
Toward an ideal and away from its unbridled rush,
Forcibly bringing it into the
Frantic, daily struggle of the present...

It seems to me that people on the street
Are engaged in a fierce battle with time,
And that, at every moment, from triumph to triumph,
They are raising an army for the future...

All while I, far from that sacred struggle,
Hide out in my thoughts, like a traitor...
Now, my conscience stricken, I dart outside in anguish,
Toward the masses, to offer my soul to the masses once and for all.

5 December, 1933
Paris

Those Deprived of Work

"Bread or work, work or bread..."
Bursting from countless, innumerable chests,
It resounds without fail from street to street,
The stubborn demand of those deprived of work.

Faces nourished by indolence, gorged on it,
Whorish thoughts perpetually indifferent,
They watch life, roused for a moment
By the sublime cry of protest and rage.

Like moles, frightened, bewildered,
Emerging suddenly from their dark burrows,
They search for a way into their own consciences,
Because for them exposure to light means certain death.

"Bread or work, work or bread..."
Even the cobblestone street is outraged,
While the *law*, uncertain and even stone-like,
Wants to hinder these crazed appeals...

Faces aged by continuous labour,
Those who for years have built our world,
Are not demanding rest
But rather fair wages and work to live.

Fresh-faced and full of life, young, strong, and
Not yet in bloom, they are being ravaged by hunger...
Oh, cynical human irony,
You have only burdened life with suffering.

"Bread or work, work or bread..."
Let us roar, comrades, our fury ablaze,
Let our surly hearts burn endlessly,
Let our demand grow like a torrent,

So that all aloof minds,
So that this worn, illegitimate world of ours,
Razed by the flames of our dense wrath,
Will eventually be entirely reduced to ash.

10 September, 1933
Alfortville
Written on the occasion of a protest

The Seamstresses

A gift to the Armenian seamstresses of Paris

By the time the first glimmers of sunlight start rising,
They are already sitting at their machines,
Sewing without interruption until the light fades into
The bosom of the blessed night and the torpor of sleep comes.

Orders are completed quickly, and the work must be neat and
Handed over to the boss. Or else there will be nothing the next day,
And the fangs of deprivation look vicious
From behind the dark curtain of misery.

Their overlords, those scoundrels, want meticulous work.
Under the ferocious lashes of exploitation,
The seamstress—at times resisting the fatigue of exertion,
        at times yielding to it—
Trembles as she weighs her conscience against her bread.

In a civilized city, at a grand table,
These women are slaves who toil all day long,
As their lives drip away drop by drop
Like cheap elixirs of life in goblets of debauchery and decadence...

Sometimes old women fending for themselves, their hands
	already leathery,
Sometimes widows out of luck, confounded by life,
And sometimes even young women, full of hopes and dreams still
	burning bright;
They all toss their days into deprivation...

Sacred work becomes a soul-sucking demon,
From whom these drained at times optionless women make every
	effort to flee.
But he has them caught in his clutches, the clutches of daily life,
Where flights of desire are enslaved against their will...

Whenever I see the boundless light in your eyes,
Light that grows dim and vanishes in exchange for some measly
	bread each day,
Oh, my sisters, my heart bleeds silently in my chest.
I yearn to take away the exhaustion that weighs heavy on your
	shoulders.

I clench my fists and grit my teeth;
A rush of hatred and vengeance rips through my soul...
Ah, fill me up! Fill me up with your torment.
May the sacred flame of the struggle against exploitation never
	flicker out...

6 July, 1934
Paris

AVINASH SHRESTHA

Translated from Nepali by Rohan Chhetri

Avinash Shrestha, I believe, is a unique case of a 'double interloper' in Nepali poetry. In his poetry, he forged a quintessentially modern Nepali diction and imagery influenced by poets ranging from the French symbolist poets to Lorca, Neruda and Salvatore Quasimodo. Along with this, he infused a distinctly Sanskrit-heavy inflorescence – drawn from the Assamese, Urdu, Hindi and Bengali poetry of India – into the idiom of Nepali poetry that was, at the time, mired in themes of social issues. In a way, the poems in his four books of poetry, and particularly his third, *Anubhuti Yatrama* (1990), resuscitated Nepali poetry to the history and condition of its own utterance, revelling in dictions high and low, the sacred and the profane, making itself aware of its own rhizomatic linguistic relations. 'Spell', from *Anubhuti Yatrama*, exemplifies this new poetry that was necessarily syncretic, surrealist by design, and heavily influenced by the Collage poetry movement Shrestha spearheaded in Assam. 'On Descending a Fog-rimmed Mountain' and 'Song of the Five Elements' are both taken from his most recent full-length collection, *Karodoun Suryaharuko Andhakar* (2001). The poems in this collection intersect Shrestha's distinct brand of religious surrealism, perfected in his first three books, with themes of ecology and climate justice.

My Poems

Not to forget a country / but to be liberated
from the spell of your immaculate face
I used to write poems.

These days, a fire burns inside me / fire that rages
in the knowledge of oppression and suffering,
to manifest the shimmering heat of that fire
I write.

Poor

Between the berating and the bullet
Between the alms and the begging bowl
Between the mob and the slogan
Between the smile and the fangs
He is one weak word
so he endures. Bows. Bends.
Without looking them in the eyes
he skirts around the big-big words.

In his horoscope his name seems to be written already:
'Poor'.

He is that kind of gunpowder, comrades.
Dampened by hunger.
Dimmed by sorrow.
Torn, muffled.
Blamed, dulled.
Diminished, blunted.
Wrenched, stifled.

Oppressed day after day
a revolt begins to heat in him
Then one day annihilating everything around him
he explodes.

He is that kind of gunpowder, comrades.

Map of a Revolution

I'm not eager to make light
of grief. Let me sing
to the tune of the hurricane
the songs of lamentation stifled
in the chest of a Dalit man.

I'll tear this rock from the soil's sensorium.
I'll scratch loose the stones at its base
and fling them. I have given
my word to history—
where the rock has usurped this soil
there shall grow a garden.

Drunk on sacrificial blood
these rocks that want to be worshipped
like gods / I will peel
and cast them off. Son of mountain, I
pour the waters of the Brahmaputra in offering
and make an oath.

I have taken the ancient task of the soil's transformation
on my shoulders. I have carried on my two arms
the map of a revolution.

JACINTA KERKETTA

Translated by Bhumika Chawla-D'Souza from Hindi

I was introduced to Jacinta's poetry in early 2016 by a friend, Vijay K. Chhabra, a highly regarded translator based in New Delhi. He sent me a few poems and I still remember the electricity in my veins when I read the poem 'Giddh Drishti' [Vulturous Eyes], from her first book *Angor*. Since then, I find myself constantly illuminated by her deceptively simple yet distinctly powerful writing.

Translating Jacinta's poetry is like trying to lasso a majestic wild horse. One often finds that the loop misses the spirit by a hair's breadth – but when one does find the right words, the ride is exhilarating. The ability to rope in immense pathos in a handful of words is characteristic of her style – and it's her shortest poems that have been the most challenging to render into English.

Adivasi (indigenous people of India) issues and concerns are at the heart of Jacinta's poetry, and her work speaks to the human condition as a whole, which is why a city-bred translator like me has found such profound connection with her words. I owe a lifetime of gratitude to Vijay Chhabra and the late Johannes Laping for introducing me to Jacinta, her work, and her beautiful friendship.

Opposite: Jacinta Kerketta

To be killed

On seeing the armed policemen
The unarmed villagers began to run –
'Halt!' said the police – but they didn't,
For the city's language was unknown to them
Enraged, the policemen fired their guns
Killing a few village men and women.

The police don't follow the forest's language
And the police's words the Adivasis cannot comprehend
That day, the escaped villagers made the decision
To teach the city's language to their children
So that they may be saved from being killed.

Armed policemen came to the forest again
And those who now understood their words
Asked them to state their intention
And were killed again by the butts of their guns
For daring to question them this way
Some did respond to the police's interrogation
But their answers didn't come up to the expectation
They couldn't fathom on what charge were they imprisoned.

Why is no language able to save
The forest people from tyranny and oppression?
They are forever plagued by this question.
But today, they can see
That knowing or not knowing the city's language
Is indeed not the condition for being safe in the forest
The mere fact that they are in the forest
Is enough for them to be massacred.

Just like in any other corner of the world
It's enough to be an Adivasi
For Adivasis to be killed,
To be wiped out slowly, meticulously.
Just like in the United States
It's enough to be 'native'
For the remaining displaced Native Americans
To be either killed or thrown for life in prison
Just like for the Blacks to be killed
It's enough to be of dark skin.

People in clothes

Those who clothe themselves from head to toe
Came in their prim and proper garb
Tearing down the door into my home they barged
I was in my room, the bare essentials I wore
They looked at me in scorn
'Half-naked! Savage! Vulgar!' they swore.

All I wish to say to them is this:
Being savage is breaking down doors
And barging into people's homes
Before talking about decency, propriety
Just learn to first knock on the door.

JORGE LAUTEN

Translated by Shook from Portuguese

Against the backdrop of occupation and genocide unfolding with US support in Palestine, I have often thought of the pseudonymous Timorese revolutionary poet Jorge Lauten. Years ago, I translated a couple of his poems, and drafted an essay about his poetry, its role in the Timorese struggle for independence, and the mystery of his identity. Last month, I worked on the remainder of his poems over the course of two days.

Timor-Leste, also known as East Timor, is a nation of 1.3 million people, on the eastern half of the island of Timor, in Southeast Asia. The Revolutionary Front for an Independent East Timor (commonly abbreviated to Fretilin) formally declared Timor-Leste's independence from Portugal on 28 November 1975. Nine days later, on orders of the military dictator Suharto, and supported by the US, Indonesian military forces invaded the nascent democracy. The estimated number of Timorese killed during the first 12 to 15 months of Indonesian occupation range from 50,000 to 100,000.

Jorge Lauten features prominently among Timor-Leste's greatest revolutionary poets writing during the period of occupation, and yet no biographical information for the poet exists. Brazilian poet and scholar Leonardo Gandolfi notes that Lauten takes on multiple personas even in the few pages of his known work, making biographical details impossible to confirm.

In Timor-Leste, confirming the poet's identity is not just impossible, but beside the point. What matters is the poet's commitment to the liberation of the oppressed—and ours, whether as translator or reader.

Bury My Heart on Mount Ramelau

1

What am I doing in this damp wooden room in this distant country?
My eyelids clench like two blades and thwart my sleep. Far away, in
the country of Timor, in the depths of the sea, the bivalve mollusk
sweetly parts its lips and serves up the last residues of light. Oh, I too
would like not to be drowned by the cascades of this memory.

2

I squint open my eyes. Trams pass like lit cages deserted on these side
streets of Lisbon. My intention to open the shutters to the early
morning light dies. I stagger through the room. In my hand, a bottle
of cheap perfume purchased at a drugstore in Australia. Oh, I know
you would love this perfume, and I am seeing you receive it with your
adolescent smile. You would love this perfume, Elisa, if you were
alive, if they hadn›t riddled your chest with their machine guns, a
butterfly of blood drawn over your dark breasts.

3

Oh Suharto, look for the last time at the black marble of your palace
floor. You will die in the sauna of your blood. You forget that Timor's
soul is a breastplate, you forget that we are the children of the great
crocodile that crossed the ocean.

4

Tata Ramelau evaporated in the fog of gases. His spirit awaits you,
soldiers from other lands, on every corner of Dili, on every bend in
the road, in every tablet of gum you chew, sweating in fear.

5

Here I am, thinking: not even death can unite us: you die for the
order and pacification of your 27th province and we die for our
independent homeland.

6

I still remember at the end of November, a child was running on the
fine sand at the beach in Dili: what wind erased his child's footprints?
What death hindered his steps? I asked all the refugees from Jamor
after this son of mine with his eyes the colour of Timor. On each face
a map of the steps lost in the exiles' sandy wrinkles.

7

I open the damp wooden closet and put on a clean shirt given to me
in Port Darwin. I open the door to this foreign land and the January
cold cuts into my skin. I close the door as if I were burying my heart
at the peak of Mount Ramelau.

Little Ode for Nicolau Lobato

I don't know precisely the day or the hour
   you died. I don't know the location of your last
     campsite

But I am certain that the colourful fish
    in my sea of memory
crazed flung
      and killed themselves on the reefs
         of my sorrow

All night the babadok drums
    played
       and
beautiful butterflies fell their wings
     iridescent
       shattered

Blades on My Feet

My rooster has a red comb
agile with flashing blades
      on his feet

Wake me up by crowing at dawn
  in my beloved region of Lospalos
With flashing blades on my feet
    I head to the thick
      of the battle

'amor omnia vincit amor omnia vincit'

KINGA TÓTH

Translated from Hungarian by Annie Rutherford

I'd been translating the work of Kinga Tóth, a Hungarian poet who writes in Hungarian, German and occasionally English, for a number of years when, in 2021, Orban's government introduced a law banning the 'promotion of homosexuality' to minors and dramatically restricting LGBTQ+ representation in the Hungarian media. It was a chilling move. Translating this poem by Kinga – and putting queer Scottish and Hungarian poets in touch with each other for some wonderfully creative exchanges – was a small gesture of solidarity, but one that felt important. Here in the UK, Section 28 had been repealed around the time I'd started secondary school, but its effects had lingered, and the parallels between the two laws were self-evident.

Santa Muerte is a folk saint and personification of death in Mexican culture. With a following that has grown over the last 25 years or so, she is associated with protection and healing – and is revered as a protector of the LGBTQ+ community. I love this poem for the sense of joyful defiance that builds as it goes on, moving from uncertainty to bravado, from the catacombs to the rainbow rivers of Pride, insistently positioning joy at the centre of queer resistance. The final lines are a rapturous refusal to meet the oppressor with the tools of oppression, a defiant celebration of community, creativity and care.

Santa Muerte

do you live in these catacombs was your head
divided from your neck did you allow it the necklaces
certainly didn't from clavicle to chin
they reflect you whoever looks at you will be met with lightning
in your cavities in two of them we stare at ourselves are scared
of the caves touch our bones while on yours
we search for stains scratches living tissue
in you we gather do not raise your hand on the last bone of
     your finger
are our traces with which we bind our face with cloths
whoever touches us shall be met by lightning by storms
may the rain wash away the traces of his hand may the hurricane
     close his eyes
don't let him see our colours we twist our beads for ourselves
hang from our ears twist the hair into flower wreaths
on our knuckles we make rows of bells with the necklace with
     ringing feet we move
through tepito guerro mexico when we stamp
the border walls in reben fall the wire fences pile up
the men's bellowing is drowned out by the ringing the gun
     barrels are overgrown
with tendrils when we scatter flowers over the soldiers the
     priests the intercessors

MaMaMuerta mother of the love parade we dance
on your lorries carry your throne present hosts
from your chalice a rainbow river flows onto the streets
    our cars become
amphibious we would grow wings as we dance
o-ra-la-bor-a ave santa

mama muerte memento mori memento amor
amor omnia vincit amor omnia vincit

BATOOL ABU AKLEEN

Translated by Batool Abu Akleen and Cristina Viti
from Arabic

I was introduced to the poetry of Batool Abu Akleen thanks to
an Italian translation by Aldo Nicosia for an anthology of
women's poetry and art dedicated to the memory of Etel Adnan.[1]
I was impressed with this young poet's facility for close observation
and empathy and by the immediacy and vividness of her language.
(In one instance, in a poem she wrote at the age of fifteen in 2020,
she takes on the voice of a mother to describe daily life in a refugee
camp and the physical and psychic impact of the violence of borders
on adults and children alike.) Over the past few months she has
strengthened her commitment to bearing witness to the *speakable*
horror of these times, and has written a number of poems in the
glare of the humanitarian catastrophe being unleashed on Gaza;
the measured tone of her vocal delivery holds the graphic extremes
of her imagery in fine balance. Thanks to her good command
of English, we were able to work together on these translations,
our drafts and recordings travelling back and forth whenever a
connection was available, our fugitive conversations widening
against blind ferocity shrinking space and time.'

---

1 Costanza Ferrini (ed.), *Di acqua e di tempo / Of Water and Time* (San Marino:
   AIEP, 2022).

I want a grave

I want a grave with a marble tombstone
my loved ones irrigate it
they place roses on it
they weep when longing stings their eyes
their tears can't reach me
so I don't get sad.

I want a grave for myself alone
so my friends can come & talk to me
so that for the last time
I'll have the right to be an individual.

I want a grave not adjoining any other grave
so my sweetheart can grow me a paperflower tree
to shelter me from the summer sun
to dress me in a magenta cloak in spring
leaves falling on my body like a warm blanket in winter.

I want a grave in a cemetery where all of my neighbours
are people who have taken their fun with life
wrapped themselves in life
then planted two kisses on life's cheeks
& died.

I want a grave
I don't want my corpse to be
decomposing in the middle of the street.

Blazing sun

I'm burning my fingers
they're melting one after the other
slowly, as war passes slowly:
Thumb to bake bread fresh like martyrs' bodies
Forefinger I put to the little girl's lips
it warms her heart
so the dread will go & calm will ripen
Middle Finger I raise between the eyes
of the bomb that hasn't yet reached me
Ring Finger I lend to the woman who lost
her hand & her husband
Little Finger will make my peace
with all the food I hated to eat.
& another five fingers to move the blazing sun aside.
War doesn't stop
I run out of fingers.
My hands get shorter
fingers grow
my hands melt
fingers grow
my chest melts
my heart,
all of me melts
nothing remains but the fire
flowing from between death's fingers
fire may choke death
but I'm the one who's choked to death.

Milad-birth[2]

Death is coming closer
I'm not scared
I'm waiting like a mother expecting her newborn
I will scream
I will feel his head coming out of my body
before my eyes
fresh blood trickling
he will wail
my voice will be stifled
I will hold him
& run my fingers over his little head
he's still wailing
the nurses will tell me I gave birth to death
I will panic
I will kiss my baby
I will hug him & crush the breath out of him
I will cry
I will weep
as he grows silent
I killed death
I killed my baby

2 'Milad' ('birth') is often used as a boy's name. The double title of this poem
   speaks the psychic short circuit experienced when acts of life take place in
   an environment relentlessly exposed to death & destruction.

LILIANA ANCALAO

Translated by Leo Boix from Spanish

'I write to remember who I am, because I was born not knowing who I was', wrote Liliana Ancalao in an essay called 'I Write to Purge This Memory'.[1] 'I write to honour the kongen, owners of the water, who came to me in the voice of my grandmother, Roberta Napaiman, when the Ngen[2] was the horse jutting his head out from a lake in Cushamen, the sound birthing a fear in us and impeding our games on the shore'.

Ancalao, a poet and activist born in Comodoro Rivadavia, a city in the Patagonian province of Chubut in southern Argentina, explores the complexities of her Mapuche identity, language, and cosmovision in her work. She also questions and challenges the violence committed against her people by the state during the Conquest of the Desert (1833–1834) and the Occupation of Araucanía (1861–1883), two military campaigns that resulted in the deaths of thousands of Mapuche people and the displacement of many more. This violence, which the Mapuche continue to endure, has persisted to this day.

I came across Ancalao's work while researching poets from Latin America who write in indigenous languages for a project commissioned by the Poetry Translation Centre (PTC) in London. After reading her first two poetry collections, *Tejido con lana cruda* (2001) and *Mujeres a la intemperie-pu zomo wekuntu mew* (2009),

1   'I Write to Purge This Memory', by Liliana Ancalao, translated from Spanish by Liliana Ancalao & Seth Michelson, published in *The Open Wound: Five Mapuche Texts* (Words Without Borders, March 2023).
2   Ngen: a spiritual entity that cares for specific people and places, sometimes becoming visible by adopting various forms.

Opposite: Liliana Ancalao

I was captivated by her unique poetic voice, her focus on her maternal language, Mapudungun, and her vivid imagery.

The poems I translated are from her first collection and appear to be a form of resistance and defiance against the state's oppression of her people, language and culture. As the poet explained in her essay, 'I write to know what death and what life I come from and endure'.

When I Die I Will Have To Cross The River

When I die I will have to cross the river
What dog will be my guide if I don't have
a scrawny dog that will smell my cowardice
it'll go by my side

And the old woman will be on the raft
I'll give her two llankas[3]
to cross over
The stones pulled out by the roots
from my throat
from my stomach
grown in the pains
in the screams I couldn't scream
when my eyes got bigger
and I pretended to live

I'll give those stones
and there will be no more
tears for sure
because I couldn't find the secret to this life
because I went
after ghosts
looking for plots
and spiders
and jugs
and leaves

3   A female personal adornment worn by Mapuche women.

Will the old woman recognise their value?
I'll get on with my dog
The raft will glide in the afternoon
to the west

we will arrive
and my little sister must be there
she has to be
death can't be nothing for a bird
for one who has painted the fire with brushes
she will have visible scars in her eyes
her eyes even more certain
will dig into me
until they pull out my thorns
she will draw my face with her fingers
an imprint of choique[4]
fire will burn on blue stones
we will eat beating hearts
and my sister will paint a kultrún[5] in the air
with blood

then I won't know
if I am a horse
or a gasp
if the wind is a trutruka[6].

4   A South American racer bird, which inhabits an area from Patagonia
    to the high plateau.
5   Ritual percussion instrument.
6   An aerophone instrument used by the Mapuche people.

and we'll gallop away

to scatter the stars of the river
and in the circular motion
I'll know at once
what it is to be a warrior running free towards death
what visions burned him

We'll return to the mallín[7]
and there will be people around the fire
the blackened pots and the moon
and every leaf of the poplars glowing

Then, I will remember myself
as them so far away
and die again

because of the housing plan neighbourhoods
growing in vertigo
in the city with a horizon
the nylon bags and the stars there
between the street lighting wires.

7   Mallín is a meadow and wetland found in southern Chile and Argentina.

question

we will have to resign ourselves to being a question
roll up our sleeves
keep walking
with a seismic shock in the back
without foundations
nor contemplations

we'll have to get used to it without an answer
to die in a story and another story
to go out mother kicking the questions
through the pipes of the skin
to the bones

and walk
human no more
underpinning struggles
controlling the pulse of the earth

to look at ourselves as rubble on the map of dreams

AMELIA ROSSELLI

Translated by Roberta Antognini and Deborah Woodard
from Italian

All of Amelia Rosselli's poetry is characterised by an inner tension
between the geometry of the prosody and the freedom of the
language. It took Rosselli seven years to complete the process of
selecting poems for *Document*. The final work, published in Milano
by Garzanti in 1976, includes 175 poems, chronologically ordered as in
Francis Petrarch's famous thirteenth century canzoniere. Long
fascinated by the classical sonnet as an ideal model, in *Document*
– her third and last major collection – Rosselli went a step further by
adopting Petrarch's approach, i.e., a text in which meaning is partially
generated by the sequence of the collection, thus helping to contain
the flood of her poetic work. At first glance, nothing seems to be
farther from *Document* than Petrarch's carefully built collection.
However, Rosselli was aware of the interplay between autobiography
(albeit highly idealised) and fiction in Petrarch's poetry, and she was
fascinated by what it means to tell a story through a collection of
poems. In Rosselli's story or stories, as in Petrarch, autobiography
is always knowingly lurking. Speaking of *Document*, Rosselli said:
'It was hard work, those who do not write poetry cannot imagine what
difficult studies poets do to compose'. This 'hard work', one Rosselli
was most fond of, resulted in the transformation of the literary model
of her predecessor Petrarch into an innovative and ambitious venture
reflecting the challenges of her own subjective experience: the pain,
the intensity and turmoil of her existence and of our own violent
and chaotic times.

General Strike 1969

brightest lamps and in the howl
of a quiet rambunctious crowd
to be there and take it seriously: that is
to risk! may in the apparent
childishness crash even my
power of not giving a damn.

An innermost God could be enough
my selfishness wasn't enough for me

wasn't enough for these people
the taste of riches in a choked

revenge after all. We had to
express the best: treat yourself

to a rhetoric that was howl
of protest at a fearless

destruction in our frightened
homes. (I lost it myself that
vertical love, solitary god
revolutionizing myself in people
removing myself from the sky.)

He too hanged the revolution
you'd like to be done with greatness
one good turn deserves another and with simplicity
(revised at one in the morning and with
insomnia) you destroy a shred
of what you'd like to destroy.

The bottom of the day is that one
they wanted to celebrate the
fifth anniversary of the victory
they convinced even you that you've gone
to drown, no one
nearby prevailed, but perished.

Dozens perished
you'll perish the next day

if you fly,
and I baptize you the enemy of the people.

Not a simple sentence
it's up to you to do without it
and thus undoing
that lesson in practicality you gave me
and punctual showing you that I too have
faith in reason.

Verses made in a furor of distraction
existed empty and vain in my mind
they show that in the end there was this
piece of paper.

The angels are leaving
white and blue
and I sit on the balcony
black and white

Crisis of bovarism
crisis of impoverishment!
crisis of flowers
crisis of workers

Four-way dialogue
like a diagonal
I describe buses
I get back on track
other prayers
why are trees blue?

(Things themselves
sow my heart with light)

RAÚL ZURITA

Translated by Jessica Sequeira from Spanish

Reading the essays of Raúl Zurita, the continuous engagement of the Chilean poet with the ancient Hindu story of the Mahabharata is apparent. The essay here, 'La enloquecedora posibilidad de la dicha', was published in *El País* in 2022, but one can find references to the Hindu story in the essays 'El tratado del llanto', 'A pleno día. El universo en paz de las escrituras' and many others, written across decades.

A tragedy of conscience and consciousness, the most famous section of the work is the Bhagavad Gita, which recounts the tale of a man who kills another that he later learns is his own brother, something fate has (maybe) decreed must occur but still makes him suffer. It is unclear whether this account of the battle, and the hell and paradise that follow, are illusions, dreams or lucid realities, and whether such euphoria and pain is inescapable, or could have been avoided. What one can control is only one's response to events.

Zurita, in the face of tortures, injustices and crushing acts of mass violence, insists on a profound, boundless love when faced with what hurts – a turning of the cheek, a pouring of acid on himself, an embrace of the acts that enable the 'maddening possibility of happiness' – even knowing this might be a temporary illusion. He seeks to look at suffering head-on, bathing in the *Sea of Pain*, as the title of his work at the 2017 Kochi-Muziris Biennale puts it, not just his own but that of others.

At the heart of the poet's reflections is an insistence on responding to incomprehensible hate (how could the gods permit this?) with the ongoing attempt to create tenderness and gentle understanding, even amidst – overwhelming – suffering, as the cries of past and myth collapse into the tragedies of the present, within the silent rectangle of a screen.

The Maddening Possibility of Happiness

For the victims, all wars are simultaneous, and in that endless
carousel of images the television shows us – news programs, direct
transmissions, commentaries, debates – we realise that those beings
we see fleeing, agonising, dying, are not fake news, just as the people
who are being murdered by the missile that is killing them are not.
Everything can be fake news, but not the fallen, not the bomb that
grinds up a child, not the face of the father screaming by his side.

These are images of desolation. In one of them, a group of first
responders travels through a peripheral neighbourhood of Kiev
carrying food and giving a little company to those prostate beings,
now impossible to evacuate and surviving amidst the rubble of the
underground metro. In one of those metros, a very old woman,
almost blind, tries to get up to hear their voices and takes one of their
hands. Everything lasts only a few moments. In the end, when she
feels that the hand is pulling away from hers, she starts to cry and
asks the first responder to stay a little longer, because the only thing
she has is the warmth of other people, and that when they leave she
will be totally alone, awake all night without being able to move,
terrified as she listens to the racket of the bombs. She also told
them that this has been her home since she was born, and that she
never thought she was going to die without even a sermon.

As if that almost instantaneous image, streamed along with
millions of others on television, were already written in an
interminable saga of revenges upon revenges, we manage to glimpse
billions of other beings crying in all of the lost battles of the earth,
and among them, as if it were a dream, we see a man, who also has
begun to cry. There is nothing that unites him with the old woman in

Opposite: Raúl Zurita

the outskirts of Kiev, save for the belonging of both to the universal community of pain.

He is named Arjuna, and he is one of the heroes of the Mahabharata, that infinite poem that constitutes one of the trunks of Hinduism. The war has been endless, and in one chapter we see two enormous armies, separated only by a valley. The start of the battle is imminent. Arjuna is the supreme commander of one of them, and all at once, looking over the valley, he feels a profound affliction for all those who are going to die there. He begins to cry. By his side is Krishna, the god-made-man, who guides his chariot of battle and who upon seeing him, says to him: 'Arjuna, do not cry, because you will believe that you are killing your enemy and your enemy will believe that he is being killed by you, but both of you will be wrong, for what does not have start does not have an end, and what has never been born cannot die.'

This is only the cry of a man, but independent of our cultures, languages and beliefs, there is something astonishing about that scene. It is as if those unfulfillable magnitudes of life, illusion and death had been written because in their tangle, the fullness of our existence is represented. We intuit for a second that there exist infinities of worlds within this world and that the devastated cities we trusted in the past are the same devastated cities that await us in the future, as if that which we have denominated history were nothing but the reiteration of an error.

And then we see the countless images of suffering, mutilation and death that human beings commit against other human beings, and amidst the storm of news, denials and nuclear threats, we realise that what we are looking at are flat images, not the plain of a valley that separates two armies, but the plain of a television screen, and that behind it, there are living displays of horror and pain, and that all of us, our bodies and our mouths, are intermingled in that rubble, in those ruins, in those faces that cry or shout...

In an inscrutable past or future, an old woman, almost blind, awake for a few seconds in the midst of her agony, feels a hand that keeps taking hold of hers, that has not left it alone, and she listens to the sermon beside her that will unite her to the immemorial chain of life and death. Deep down, all battles have ceased, and the two armies that were going to confront each other dissolve.

But this is no more than a dream; the dream of the maddening possibility of happiness.

'My front
façade is
autumn'

YI SANG

Translated by Jack Saebyok Jung from Korean

'Destruction of Texts' is a translation of a posthumous poem by Korean modernist, and multi-genre artist, Yi Sang (1910–1937). Published in October 1937, a few months after the poet's untimely death, the poem's Korean title is 파첩(破帖). There are various ways to translate this unusual combination of literary Chinese characters, which Yi Sang often employed in his poetry. My chosen translation is one such interpretation, while another could be 'Destroyed (or Torn) Notebook.'

In South Korea, opinions on the poem's meaning have been diverse, as is the case with much of Yi Sang's work. This piece strikingly addresses the theme of a destroyed urban landscape, and recent scholarship suggests that this may reflect Yi Sang's work as an architect for Japan's colonial government in Korea before he became a writer. He might have been involved in urban planning that led to the destruction of old neighbourhoods as Seoul modernised to accommodate Japanese businesses and homes. In this sense, the poem can be read as a confession of the speaker's guilt. Yet, as a colonised subject, Yi Sang's guilt is also layered with his own victimisation, positioning him as both victim and perpetrator.

Encountering this poem today, its scenes of urban ruin and warfare evoke the chilling reality in Gaza. The original context of the poem, alongside its contemporary relevance, underscores how little has changed and highlights the continuing need for progress.

Destruction of Texts

1

Imagine, an elegant lady thief stalking me.
My door's latch is my howl, the frozen recording of my fleeting
    thoughts, or another layer of my thoughts...
—How can you be so heartless—
The lamplight is dim, and the lady thief's milky body is bewitchingly
    profane—or pure.

2

Battle is over in the city. The sidewalks are littered with untangled hemp.
    Following orders, moonlight splashes its ink on this hemp-littered
    place.
(O be a protective colour) I imitate what is happening haha ha!

3

Many people have died, but almost no corpse has been left behind.
    Ghastly cannon blasts secretly raise humidity. The living of the
    world no longer germinates. Dark night continues in
dark night.
At last, the monkey falls into deep sleep. The air is powdered
    milky white.
Me?
On my way back home, I step on dead bodies, raising the hair on
    my skin. From far behind me, I can hear myself reading a book.

4

Why is there a postal service in this capital's ruin?
Huh? (Please be quiet, it is the crone's vulva)

5

On a sheet, my faint outline is printed. Anatomical chart does not
take my skull into its consideration.

My front façade is autumn. Near the foliage, a transparent flood
subsides.

After sleep, my fingertips get cold from sulfuric urination.
A dewdrop finally falls.

6

While walking, I see continental girls on the second floor of a
building, closing their windows.

They spit before closing.

As if they are firing at me.

I think about what will happen inside and feel envy. I lean my
blushing body on the building's wall and investigate that spit.
The lewd

foreign words are filled within,

wriggling like germs.

In a boudoir, I raise a cripple by myself. The cripple sometimes
suffocates. Blood flow hesitates.

7

I hide my button. I do not sign in public... where, where do the
assassins spend their nights like owls? No one knows.

8

...The sidewalk's microphone sends its last electrical current over
wire.

Moonlight excavates the dark night—

Dead bodies are colder than their lost body heat, even though frost
has come down on their ash...

Suddenly, a ruined steel plate falls, but its stubborn noise leaves
no vibration.
Underneath, an old assemblyman, and an old professor, give lecture,
again and again.
"What must come with what?"
Their faces look like the faces of their predecessors.
In an empty station, a truck is tall and proud, and it is going to.

9

Is it the secret code with a medal? It rides on the electrical currents,
and commands Canaan of annihilation.
The collapse of the city is—ah!—faster than the rumors blowing in
the wind.

10

The city hall hid the book of laws and denied chaotic disposal.
In the "concrete" countryside, there are no herbal roots, nor tree
barks. There is no life even in
the shadow of an object.
—Cain, the lonely engineer, will push and pull his rickshaw in front
of the city's gate. And he
will always slowly walk these streets.

INGEBORG BACHMANN

Translated by Alexander Stillmark from German

Ingeborg Bachmann, one of the foremost poets of postwar German literature, wrote in vehement protest against the recent historical past. Her early lyric poems soon established her reputation as the leading voice of her generation. Her deeply felt antagonism to the brutal, inhuman era of the Third Reich made her a stranger in her native Austria and she spent much of her adult life in Italy and France. As a poet she experienced her situation in society as one of isolation and sorrow, yet one where militant opposition to social ills becomes the necessary response. Her poetic diction bears the mark of a profoundly sentient intellect which is balanced by a natural, inspired use of figurative language. The need for a purified, lucid poetic language, freed from the polluted political jargon of the past, is a driving mechanism of her creativity.

Psalm

1

Keep silent with me, just as all bells are silent!

In the afterbirth of terrors
the vermin seek new fodder.
On some good Fridays a hand hangs for show
upon the firmament, two fingers short,
it cannot swear on oath that all of this,
all of this never occurred and that nothing
is to come. It dips into cloud-crimson,
removes the new murderers
and goes free.

By night upon this earth
to grope through windows, to turn back the sheets,
that the patients' secrecy is laid bare,
a festering sore to feast on, unending agony
for every taste.

The butchers, gloved and ready,
stifle the breath of those exposed,
the moon in the doorway crashes to earth,
let the shivers lie there, the handle...

All was made ready for extreme unction.
(The sacrament cannot be performed.)

2

How futile everything is.
Heave along a whole town,
arise from the dust of that town,
assume an office
and affect a pose
to evade exposure.

Make good all promises
before a darkened mirror in the air,
before a bolted door in the wind.

Untrodden are the paths over the rock face of the heavens.

3

O eyes, burnt by the sun-store of earth,
oppressed by the rain-freight of all eyes,
and now involved, ill-woven
by the tragic spiders
of the present...

4

Into the hollow of my muteness
place a word
and foster forests on either side,
that my mouth
may lie wholly in shade.

And follows us up to the mouth of the river.

To Speak Darkly

Like Orpheus I play
Death upon the strings of life
and into earth's beauty
and your eyes, which govern heaven,
I can but speak darkly.

Never forget that you also, all at once,
on that morning, while where you lay
was still wet with dew and the carnation
slept by your heart,
also saw the dark river
flowing past you.

The strings of silence
strung on the billow of blood,
I plucked your sounding heart.
Your locks were transformed
into the shadow-hair of night,
the black flakes of gloom
snowed on your countenance.

And I do not belong with you.
We now both lament.

Yet like Orpheus I know
life's on the side of death,
and to me your eyes eternally closed
shine blue.

ABD AL-KARIM AL-AHMAD

Translated by Catherine Cobham from Arabic

The personification of the surging waves makes them appear like a monster coming after you. This renders the waves both intimate and familiar, like the stuff of fairy tales. However, very quickly, this illusion is shattered by the images that dramatise the absolute powerlessness of the protagonists/victims. The 'you' is a plural pronoun in Arabic. (This is conveyed slightly awkwardly in line 6 of the translation by the 'all' ['you all will be the baseballs'].) The protagonists can expect no help, from either ineffectual deities or the inadequate man-made infrastructure. They are up against the enemy, at 'distance zero', which I imagine is an ironic reference to AI. The boat is briefly personified, giving us a more explicit context – migrants in small boats – but almost at once, it vanishes as even its memory is erased, swallowed up by the surprisingly dexterous waves. Only in the last few lines does the narrator identify himself as a participant in the action as he introduces a drowned or drowning person. Whether this person was swept away by the waves or is deliberately moving away (to spare his companions?) is unclear, and we are left with his companions' helpless disbelief.

The last few lines are uncomfortable and ambiguous in the original, and may come across as awkward and less convincing in the translation. In any case, the poem is able to say more about the infamous 'small boats' than many news items.

Distance Zero

You will be chased by waves that perfect the art of impossible descents
They will see you with a resolution of 30 megapixels
And you will hear the ringing of their hidden bells
They will fly at an altitude impossible to calculate
A terrifying erection of watery swords
They will be the hammers and you all will be the baseballs
And from distance zero they will fire blind showers of watery lava
You will ask for help from rescue cells
And from the god who studies available options
Do not seek safe havens
There are no buffer zones or borders fortified with cement barriers
Those waves that yawn profoundly
Will erase the memory of the boat that lost its sense of security
Then they will disappear into invisible sewers
Relying on the flexibility of their spinal column
I too was there
In the same whirlpool
And the drowning person was moving away from us
Maybe against his will, maybe not
But he did it anyway
And still we refuse to believe

MOISEI FISHBEIN

Translated by John Hennessy and Ostap Kin from Ukrainian

The poet Paul Celan left Chernivtsi, his hometown in the region of
Bukovyna, where he spent twenty-five years of his life (minus those
years in a labour camp during the Second World War), sometime in
the spring of 1945. The poet Moisei Fishbein was born in Chernivtsi
one year later, in 1946. One can't just ignore these biographical
details; they highlight the rapid and metaphysical transformation of
a city, leading to a transformation of the poets inhabiting or leaving
that city. A poet working in the German language was forced to
flee and was superseded by another poet, who opted to work in
Ukrainian. Both of them could have selected other languages, but
they did not – and they had their reasons for that. In some sense,
their language remains the same: it's the language of poetry.

Unwilling to cooperate with the KGB, Fishbein had little choice
but to escape. He left the Soviet Union in 1978. Shortly before his
imposed departure, Fishbein composed these two poems. They are
directly related to Paul Celan, written in dialogue with Celan, written
for Celan, and written in Celan's city. Fishbein's poems showcase a
deep connection with the poet, whom he also rendered into
Ukrainian – a fact that creates another layer of conversation. These
poems are testament to one poet engraving the memory of another
poet into a different culture and to the work against one's 'unrooting'
from what Czeslaw Milosz once called 'native lands'. It's a dissent
against a forced and imposed custom of non-remembrance or
un-remembrance practised in the Soviet Union.

In Memory of Paul Celan

A master of sticks and shuttered glass,
a wet memento of withered roots,
a disoriented bird, an autumn song,
and in her throat a little algae blooms—

above him the cold burden of water,
and twinkling in his eyes, a green sun.
O inviolable mobile surface!
O fragile headstone with no inscription!

A lonely child immersed in desert night.
From water into infinity a voice quietly blooms,
and sounds like shadows echo above the water—

an inaudible shadow will cover the small city.
Through detached and dark oblivion
his young eyes will watch attentively.

[it's still a wheel, the well still at rest]

To Mykola Lukash

...and then it was a wheel,
it no longer sings with you
in the chorus of native voices...

Paul Celan

...it's still a wheel, the well still at rest,
still the lure of vertical darkness,
the roots of night, the flickering candlelight
with an imprint of primordial dust.

...it's still a wheel, all traces forgotten still,
voices still lost in the earth,
still abysses separating gazes,
still the river of blood you cross.

...it's still a wheel, a boat, a migratory bird,
a forgotten spear in perpetual launch,
the fog, Pontic wind across your temples,
still, the silence of a prayer on your lips...

EMIL-IULIAN SUDE

Translated from Romanian by Diana Manole

Avoiding both self-victimisation and explicit socio-political activism, Emil-Iulian Sude's poetry is defined by an organic mixture of irony, existential reflection, the search for identity, and concerns about human rights, and ethnic discrimination. Surrealist images are often built with everyday details, suggesting a literary style that I have previously identified as 'magic naturalism' (*Asymptote*, Winter 2022). Both Sude, the individual, and the first-person speaker in his poems belong to the Roma ethnic minority. Enslaved in Eastern Europe, and specifically until 1856 in Romania, Roma have been discriminated against, feared, derisively stereotyped, mistreated or ignored ever since.

As a security guard at a public school in Bucharest, Sude also reflects on classist stereotyping, especially in the collection *The Night Security Guard at Night* (Laertes Press, US, forthcoming in 2025 in my English translation), from which these poems are excerpted. As Sude sees them, the security guards are neither dead nor alive; they are invisible to everyone but their supervisor, and are easily replaceable. In 'They leave us jobless in the dead of winter', for example, Sude uses 'guraiernii' [the mouth of the winter], which is more closely associated with dying of hunger than of the cold in Romanian villages. This metaphorical connection is lost in translation, even if I've been able to preserve the idea of dying. Finding the best solutions can be a fascinating and rewarding task in the attempt to introduce English readers to Roma literature from Romania in general, and Sude's poetry in particular.

They leave us jobless in the dead of winter

but we don't complain. we'll always
find something to guard. we'll even build
a site to guard to have it
just for us. to be site supervisors
to guard us from ourselves
sometimes when spring kicks off to
blossom on the mirabelle plum trees
if at least the nettles sprout

we open our mouths those clay pots. we can't
even sit and do nothing in the cracks of the pavement anymore or
wait for a spark to fall from the sky.

nobody knows how. in the dead of winter hunger's teeth
bite into the warm blood we still have a secret life of our own.
our ties to the dream
in which it's late summer. determined to untie us.

We smoke a cigarette we smoke a loaf of bread

the cigarette's crust that part a little darker
and crispier. snapping between our fingers
when we squeeze it with the hills of
the palm. what a scratchy slide when you break it
off the body. and what a hunger it hides.
a slice of bread a slice of hunger
just watch how our mouths meet
and we talk about this and that
each of us in the mouth of the other. we chew ourselves
we soak ourselves in saliva to blow smoke
through all the pores those wheat straws grow.
nothing grows close to these tobacco plants. but we
imagine some chopped leaves
wrapped in newspaper pages full of lead.
nothing grows close to us. nothing
there's almost nothing left of the cigarette butts
in the sand bucket.
through every pore we blow a slice of hunger
which costs as much as a cigarette.

GHAZAL MOSADEQ

Translated by Khashayar "Kess" Mohammadi from Persian

More than anything, Ghazal Mosadeq's *Andarznama*, from which
these poems are excerpted, is an experiment in the immediacy of the
vernacular. Mosadeq's writing here is speech battling interruptive
waves of thought, through speech. For me as a translator, the most
important task has been to thoroughly preserve the immediacy of the
interruptions. The translation therefore tries to reflect the same
self-referential and self-aware poetics that Mosadeq has produced in
the original Persian text. The focus here, therefore, becomes not so
much the careful choice of words, but a careful choice of flow that
can reproduce the same ease of interruptive speech of the original.

we found the stairway behind the building   the weeds grown over cracked
rock
                    the round particles of sunlight   the shadow of the leaf
                                        a dirty broken glass
          dust—
the threat of dying alone when our children   – and their children
                                        have not been there
                          for years

we found it all   names of objects   their geometry
what we claimed to be fear   but later found to be excitement
we found it all

if they'd let us   just one more time   we'd perhaps find ourselves too
—passersby from behind—   we'd   drag the torn-apart bag filled with
pumpkins
to the end of the street   we'd find a language where we could greet
warmly
but explain no more

it's possible right now but—   a group of people are killing another group of people
right now
we found rays of light on the stairwell   it wasn't the best time

Opposite: Ghazal Mosadeq

this Saturday will be the day they call the midpoint of life
– and that's for all of us –   we found the silence they claimed to envelop all
          little by little   amidst conversations   arranged the retrieved
pieces side by side
the empty spaces weren't us   — well they were and were not—
particles of light and the glass filled it perfectly   say the light and the glass
perfectly complement the silence

                                        *

they were smoking on balconies—   these past occupiers of these streets
sweet dreams,   —sweet dreams.
          I hope you see warm tea in waking life,   —a breakfast
having slept the night before   —having seen sweet dreams

when you wake in the morning, the bus has already gone—   you
          didn't even need to be there

          I hope   —the morning is an off day
the clouds come   the clouds go
          —as you wake

NOTES ON CONTRIBUTORS

ABD AL-KARIM AL-AHMAD was born in Syria and currently lives in Germany. He writes poetry, short stories and social blogs. His works have been translated into various European languages.

ADAM PIETTE is Professor at the University of Sheffield and is the author of books on modernism and war studies, and co-edits *Blackbox Manifold* with Alex Houen. His poetry collection *Nights as Dreaming* was published by Constitutional Information in 2023. He's currently working on translations of Attila József with Ágnes Lehóczky.

AFRIZAL MALNA is a poet, artist, critic, and playwright. His work has won a number of awards, and he has performed at poetry festivals throughout Europe and Asia.

ÁGNES LEHÓCZKY is a poet, academic and translator; her most recent collection *Lathe Biosas*, or *on Dreams and Lies* was published by Crater Press in 2023. She is Senior Lecturer in Creative Writing and Director of the Centre for Poetry and Poetics, University of Sheffield. She's currently working on translations of Attila József with Adam Piette.

ALEXANDER STILLMARK is Emeritus Reader at University College London. He has, on three occasions, been awarded the Translation Prize of the Austrian Federal Chancellor's Office. His translations of Georg Trakl and Turgenev appeared in MPT nos. 8, 11 and 16. His previous translations of Ingeborg Bachmann appeared in MPT no. 3, (2022).

ALI ASADOLLAHI, an Iranian poet, is the author of six Persian poetry books. Asadollahi is a permanent member of the Iranian Writers' Association (founded in 1968). His poems and translations are published/forthcoming in *Consequence*, *Denver Quarterly*, *Epoch*, *Hayden's Ferry Review*, *Hypertext*, *Los Angeles Review*, and others.

AMELIA ROSSELLI (1930–1996) was the daughter of anti-Fascist activists, a trilingual writer who described herself as 'a poet of exploration'. *Document* (1969) is her longest collection.

ANNIE RUTHERFORD makes things with words, and champions poetry and translation in all its guises. She is a translator, writer and project leader based in Edinburgh and is working towards setting up a writers in exile residency in Scotland. Her translations include collections by German/Swiss poet Nora Gomringer and Belarusian poet Volha Hapeyeva.

ATTILA JÓZSEF (1905–1937) is one of the most renowned Hungarian poets of the 20th century who gained recognition for his literary achievement only after his tragic death in 1937. He is one of the best known of the modern Hungarian poets internationally.

AVINASH SHRESTHA was born in Guwahati, India, and moved to Kathmandu in 1990. His most recent full-length collection, *Karodoun Suryaharuko Andhakar* [Darkness of a Million Suns] was published in 2001. He has received the Mainali Katha Purashkar, the Nepal Motion Picture Award, the Dhaulagiri Sahitya Puraskar (for the poetry collection *Anubhuti Yatrama*), and the Yuva Barsha Moti Puraskar, among others.

BATOOL ABU AKLEEN is an award-winning Palestinian poet and painter. One of the top students at IUG in Gaza, she was displaced during the invasion of her country in October 2023, but continues writing and sharing her work.

BHUMIKA CHAWLA-D'SOUZA is a professional freelance translator with nearly 25 years of experience. Born and raised in Delhi and now based in Bangalore, she transitioned from a corporate career to freelance translation. She works with German, English, and Hindi, and knows a smattering of Marathi, Konkani and Kannada. She lives with her husband and five beloved dogs.

CATHERINE COBHAM taught Arabic at St Andrews for many years. She has translated the work of a number of Arab writers, including Mahmoud Darwish and Naguib Mahfouz.

CRISTINA VITI's recent publications include Pasolini's *La rabbia* (Tenement Press, 2022) and *An Anarchist Playbook* (NoUP, 2024), a series of texts co-translated in her workshop at King's College.

DANIEL OWEN is a poet, editor, and translator between Indonesian and English. Recent publications include a revised translation of Afrizal Malna's *Document Shredding Museum* (World Poetry Books, 2024).

DEBORAH WOODARD is a poet and translator. With *Roberta Antognini*, she has translated Amelia Rosselli's *Hospital Series*, *Obtuse Diary*, *The Dragonfly*, *Notes Scattered and Lost* (forthcoming), and *Document* (forthcoming).

DIANA MANOLE is a proudly hyphenated Romanian-Canadian writer, translator, and scholar. Her translations have been published on five continents and earned her 2nd prize at Dryden and *Lunch Ticket*'s Gabo prize.

EMIL-IULIAN SUDE is one of the first award-winning poets of Roma ethnicity in Romania. *The Night Security Guard at Night* is forthcoming (tr. Diana Manole) from Laertes Press (US) in 2025.

GHAZAL MOSADEQ is a poet, editor and translator. She is the founder of Pamenar Press, an independent publisher of poetry, translation, hybrid and critical writing. Her own work has been published by *Shearsman*, *Fence*, *Arc Poetry*, *Firmament*, *Asymptote* and *Words Without Borders*, among others. She is a member of the editorial advisory board for the *Journal of British and Irish Innovative Poetry*.

HENRI-MICHEL YÉRÉ (b. 1978, Abidjan, Côte d'Ivoire) is an historian based at the Centre for African Studies at the University of Basel. Yéré has published three books of poetry. His poems and articles have appeared across various journals.

HUSSEIN BARGHOUTHI (1954–2002) was a Palestinian poet, philosophy teacher, songwriter, autobiographer and saint. His body was consumed by leukemia in 2002 during the Second Intifada, but his spirit remains alive in Palestine's rocks, its light, its almond trees.

INGEBORG BACHMANN (1926–1973) was born in Klagenfurt, Karinthia, Austria. She studied philosophy at the universities of Innsbruck and Graz, completing a doctorate on Martin Heidegger in 1949. In 1952 the Gruppe 47 awarded her their annual literary prize. Her first collection of verse *Die gestundete Zeit* appeared in 1953. She was closely associated with a number of important contemporary artists inluding Paul Celan, Thomas Bernhard and Hans Werner Henze.

JACINTA KERKETTA was born in the Oraon Adivasi community of West Singhbhum district of Jharkhand. She is a poet, writer, award-winning journalist, and activist. Her writing and work primarily discuss the trials and tribulations of the Adivasi community in India and globally.

JACK SAEBYOK JUNG is 2024 NEA Translation Fellow and is currently working on translating Kim Hyesoon's hybrid collection *Thus Spoke n't*. He studied at the Iowa Writers' Workshop where he was a Truman Capote Fellow. He is a co-translator of *Yi Sang: Selected Works* (Wave Books 2020). He teaches at Davidson College.

JENNIFER MANOUKIAN is a translator and historian of Armenian social and intellectual life in the Ottoman Empire and post-genocide diaspora.

JESSICA SEQUEIRA is a writer and literary translator. Her works include *Golden Jackal/Chacal Dorado*, *Other Paradises: Poetic Approaches to Thinking in a Technological Age*, *A Luminous History of the Palm*, *A Furious Oyster* and *Rhombus and Oval*. She has translated over twenty-five books of fiction, non-fiction and poetry, mostly by Latin American authors. Her musical group Lux Violeta creates music with lyrics from poetry and Asian and Latin American rhythms.

JIKE AYOU was born in Puge County of Sichuan Province, and is the first migrant worker poet of Yi ethnicity. He is one of six poets featured in *The Verse of Us*, a documentary film on Chinese migrant worker poets. His collection of poems *All of Our Homecomings Are Feted as Yi New Year* was published by Taibai Literature and Art Publishing House in 2019.

JOHN HENNESSY's most recent collections include *Exit Garden State*, poems, and *Set Change*, Selected Poems by Yuri Andrukhovych, translated with Ostap Kin, both forthcoming in 2024.

JORGE LAUTEN is you.

KHASHAYAR "KESS" MOHAMMADI is a queer, Iranian born, Toronto-based poet, writer and translator. They are the author of four poetry chapbooks, three translated poetry chapbooks, and two full-length collections of poetry. Their full-length collaborative poetry manuscript *G* came out with Palimpsest Press in fall 2023, and their full-length collection of experimental dream-poems *Daffod*ls* is out with Pamenar Press (2023).

KINGA TÓTH is a writer, visual and sound-poet, performer and translator writing in Hungarian, German and English. In 2020, Kinga Tóth received the Hugo Ball Förderpreis for her intermedial literary work in German and she has also received the Bernard Heidsieck Prix (by Centre Pompidou and Foundation Bonotto) for her performative literary work.

KI-TYO SSEMMA'NDA was born in Uganda and went to school in Leeds, UK. His wrote his debut social justice poems called *Colored Armpits*, 2016 (Archway Publishers). Ki-tyo currently lives in Boston, USA.

LEO BOIX is a bilingual Latinx poet and translator born in Argentina who lives in the UK. His second poetry collection is forthcoming with Chatto & Windus (Vintage) in June 2025.

LILIANA ANCALAO is a member of the Mapuche-Tehuelche Nankulaven community in the Patagonian province of Chubut in Argentina. She is a Mapuche poet researching Mapuche culture and indigenous music.

MOISEI FISHBEIN (1946–2020) was an award-winning Ukrainian poet, essayist, and translator. His publications include seven collections of poems as well as children's literature, literary translations and nonfiction.

MISSAK MANOUCHIAN (1906–1944) was a poet and a member of the French Resistance. A child survivor of the Armenian genocide, he immigrated to France in 1924 and joined the French Communist Party a decade later. He is best remembered today for his role in fighting against the Nazi occupation of France and for his subsequent execution by firing squad. In February 2024, Manouchian along with his wife and fellow French Resistance fighter Mélinée were recognized as French national heroes and entombed in the Panthéon in Paris.

OSTAP KIN has edited *Babyn Yar: Ukrainian Poets Respond* and *New York Elegies: Ukrainian Poems on the City* and translated, with John Hennessy, Yuri Andrukhovych and Serhiy Zhadan.

RAÚL ZURITA was born in Santiago in 1950, and studied to be an engineer specialising in metallic structures. He was an active member of the Colectivo de Acciones de Arte (CADA), which staged artistic performances during the Pinochet dictatorship. His books of poetry include *Purgatorio* (1979), *Canto a su amor desaparecido* (1985), *La vida nueva* (1994) and *Zurita* (2011), and he has published many essays and letters. Zurita participated in the 2016 Kochi-Muziris Biennale with a poem installation called 'Sea of Pain', reflecting on the deaths of immigrants in the Mediterranean Sea.

ROHAN CHHETRI is the author of *Slow Startle*, and *Lost, Hurt, or in Transit Beautiful*, winner of the Kundiman Poetry Prize. He has also co-edited *Shreela Ray: On the Life and Work of an American Master*. His poems and translations have appeared in *The Paris Review, Poetry London,* the Academy of American Poets' *Poem-a-Day*, and *Words Without Borders* among others, and has appeared in numerous anthologies like *The Forward Book of Poetry 2023* and *The Bloomsbury Anthology of Great Indian Poems*.

ROBERTA ANTOGNINI is Associate Professor Emerita at Vassar College. With Deborah Woodard, she has translated Amelia Rosselli's *Hospital Series, Obtuse Diary, The Dragonfly, Notes Scattered and Lost* (forthcoming), and *Document* (forthcoming).

SHAHIN SHIRZADI, born in 1989, has published three Persian poetry books: *Polytechnic* (2013), *Jabr-e Nabāti* [Vegetative Determinism] (2017), and *Mu'allaq Dar Davāt* [Suspended in the Ink] (2021). Shirzadi holds a PhD in linguistics and has organised various free courses in renowned universities of Iran to teach the history of modern Persian poetry.

SUNEELA MUBAYI is a translator between Arabic, Urdu and English, an independent scholar, and writer of mixed descent, whose interests stand at the juncture where language, the body, and poetry intersect.

SHOOK is a poet and translator in California. Their most recent translations include Conceição Lima's *No Gods Live Here* (Deep Vellum), Farhad Pirbal's *Refugee Number 33,333* (Deep Vellum), with *Pshtiwan Babakr*, and Víctor Terán's *The Thorn of Your Name* (Poetry Translation Centre).

TODD FREDSON is the author of several books of poetry and poetry in translation. His most recent translation, *Zakwato & Loglêdou's Peril* by Bété poet Azo Vauguy, was a finalist for the 2023 National Book Critics Circle Barrios Book in Translation Prize.

YĚ YĚ is the co-founder of Poetry Lab Shanghai, and has had two collections of poetry published. Her words have appeared in the87press, Pamenar Press, *Voice & Verse* poetry magazine and elsewhere.

YI SANG (1910–1937) was a painter, architect, and writer of 1930s Korea, when the Korean peninsula was under Japanese colonial rule. Yi Sang wrote in both Korean and Japanese until his early death from tuberculosis at the age of 27, after imprisonment by Japanese police for thought crimes in Tokyo.